I, Jane Austen

I, Jane Austen

A re-creation in rime royal
based on the letters of
Jane Austen, her novels and
the comments of her biographers

Mary Corringham

Routledge & Kegan Paul   London

By the same author
The Temple Invisible and other Poems
(Theosophical Publishing House,
Adyar, Madras, India, 1939)

Part of *I, Jane Austen* was awarded a prize in a
competition conducted by the Australian Broad-
casting Commission, and was twice broadcast
throughout Australia on the national network.

First published 1971
by Routledge & Kegan Paul Ltd
Broadway House, 68–74 Carter Lane
London EC4V 5EL
Printed in Great Britain by
Alden & Mowbray Ltd
at the Alden Press, Oxford
© Mary Corringham 1971
ISBN 0 7100 7102 7

Dedicated to the memory of
Robert William Chapman, C.B.E.
(1881–1960)
Hon. D.Litt. (Oxon.), Hon. LL.D. (St. And.), F.B.A.

whose long list of scholarly publications contains many works affording endless delight and enlightenment to students of Jane Austen's life and writings; notably his editions of her novels (1923) and of her letters (1932, 1952); of *Sanditon* (1924), *Volume the First* (1933) and *Volume the Third* (1951); together with *Jane Austen: Facts and Problems* (1948) and *Jane Austen: A Critical Bibliography* (1953).

He was the greatest Janeite of them all

Contents

Foreword

I am delighted to be able to write a few words of tribute to this poem and its author, Mary Corringham. Over and above its intrinsic qualities as a poem, it has an added fascination for all lovers of Jane Austen. Remarkably, it seems that Jane Austen's pattern of thought and wording fall naturally into the pattern of the rime royal form in which this poem is cast; and Janeites can count on their delighted recognition of Jane Austen's own words and thoughts. For some readers, there will be the added pleasure (unpoetic but permissible) of tracking down the precise source for lines and stanzas whose source or reference is not immediately recognized.

I am sure that the pleasure that I and my friends have found in *I, Jane Austen* will be shared by many more.

B. C. SOUTHAM

But come, fond Fancy, thou indulgent power;
  Hope is desponding, chill, severe, to thee:
Bless thou this little portion of an hour;
  Let me behold her as she used to be.

From Jane Austen's poem, 'To the Memory of
Mrs. Lefroy', written in 1808

I

By way of introduction

Daring to be an authoress

Letters are made of simpler stuff

Sharing life's little things
with a loved sister

I

So many friends have recently been moved
to write with pleasure of my books and me,
that I rejoice to know I'm still approved;
although it was not my philosophy
to plague myself about posterity.
I merely never wrote for such dull elves
as could not image a good deal themselves.

2

Distinction by my novels to have earned,
rather surprises me, I must confess.
Of all females, I was the most unlearned
that ever dared to be an authoress.
How uninformed I was, I wish to stress.
English, my mother tongue, was all I knew,
and of its major works had read but few.

3

A little bit of ivory was mine—
barely two inches wide, though most select!
On this I laboured with a brush so fine
as to produce with much work small effect.
Some say the narrowness they can detect.
On guilt and misery other pens might dwell:
A comfortable tale *I* chose to tell.

4

Though never letter-writing's worst addict,
I told my sister each stray thought of mine.
A judgment that I scorn to contradict,
passed by some critics, says I did not shine
brightly in the epistolary line,
because without a great amount to say
I covered pages when she was away.

5

Nobody feels, acts, suffers, or enjoys
as one expects. Yet critics startled look
whenever any authoress employs
less skill on letters than on her last book.
In penning these, I merely undertook
to use the simplest stuff at my command,
as birds build nests from twigs and moss at hand.

6

Yet I consider that I had attained
true letter-writing art, which, we are told,
is to express on paper, unrestrained,
the same thoughts that in speech we would unfold,
and nothing—great or trivial—withhold.
In letters, then, as fast as I well could
I talked of things Cassandra understood.

4 4 4

7

Cassandra was herself one of the best
of all the comic writers of the age.
The sparkling epigram, the well-turned jest,
in every letter flashed from every page.
The elder daughter of the parsonage
seldom combines with wisdom so much wit;
but here her workmanship was exquisite.

8

Cassandra once had been engaged to wed
the Reverend Thomas Fowle. By some mischance
he caught the yellow fever, soon was dead;
and thus had ended her too brief romance.
Though saddened by this trying circumstance,
my sister met it with a high degree
of resolution and propriety.

9

There was not any creature in the land
to whom I spoke with so much openness;
convinced that she would hear and understand,
and rightly all my hopes and fears assess.
Those little things on which the happiness
of daily life depends, when shared with her,
gained a more gratifying character.

 II

Tom Lefroy and his white coat

Was my heart broken?

Spirited young men and their ways

Such disappointments never kill

10

Many exceedingly good balls we had,
for when I was a girl I loved to dance.
At three, one year, I met a charming lad
called Tom Lefroy, whose ardent Irish glance
held all the promise of a high romance.
The way we danced together, and sat down
together, was the talk of the whole town.

11

Though usually a very few hours spent
in the hard labour of incessant speech
serve to dispose of every argument
within any two normal creatures' reach,
a lover's feelings different practice teach:
each subject still has much he must unfold,
and nothing's said till twenty times it's told.

12

Tom had one fault which time might have removed.
Greatly admiring Fielding's famous book,
the clothing of Tom Jones he also loved,
and for his morning coat a light one took,
that like his namesake hero he might look.
Had he proposed to me, I'd meant to say:
'Not till you've given that white coat away!'

13

Then Tom went back to Ireland without
the offer I'd expected to receive.
Was my heart broken? Even friends could doubt,
and wonder if I secretly might grieve—
it seems I'd worn my heart upon my sleeve!
But there were other good-looking young men
in Hampshire, and the fun went on again.

14

A celebrated writer has maintained
that no young lady can be justified
falling in love, till she has ascertained—
by what the gentleman dares to confide—
that *he* loves her, for whom her heart has sighed.
To dream of him, indeed, would be to err,
before he's first known to have dreamt of *her*.

15

Perhaps it would be foolish to expect
that spirited young men should be required
always to be so guarded and correct
as not to let us know we are admired.
It's our own vanity, if we're inspired
to fancy more in it than outward show—
though men, of course, take care we *should* do so.

16

Yet I believe that I have never seen
an inclination that could promise more.
The inattentive way Tom would demean
himself to other people, and forbore
to dance or talk with them, *they* might deplore;
but in its general incivility
it showed love's symptoms to acute degree.

17

Perhaps I had been too much at my ease;
had been too happy and too frank; had erred
against decorum's rigid devotees;
had been sincere and open, in a word,
instead of dull, deceitful, and unstirred.
The roads and weather, only, it would seem,
(once in ten minutes) should have been my theme.

18

Where persons wish another to attach,
they should endeavour to seem ignorant.
Woman must hide her brains to make a match,
and let the man think he is dominant.
Females, indeed, that the most men enchant,
show imbecility as their chief charm:
few men view clever girls without alarm.

19

However deeply we believe we care,
it was no creed of mine, and is not still—
as all my friends must surely be aware—
such sort of disappointments ever kill.
I don't say that they cannot make you ill!
To give a loved one up brings suffering,
from which time only can remove the sting.

20

The pain of parting from a friend is felt
by everyone at times, whatever be
their state or education. But I dwelt
not long on it. By working busily,
from my desponding thoughts I soon was free.
My daily interests were much the same;
I did not flinch at mention of Tom's name.

21

Yet though I did not shut myself away,
nor leave the house to seek for solitude,
nor lie awake at night; still every day
some moments came when I could not exclude
the thought of him, by which I was pursued.
With pity, censure, doubt, and tenderness,
he still engrossed my fancy, I confess.

III

Marrying for love and marrying
without it

The single woman

Will perfection come our way?

An appetite for enjoyment

22

I think that everybody has a right,
once in their lives to marry, if they can,
for love. But it is dreadful to unite
without affection any girl and man.
Of loveless weddings I'm no partisan.
Anything I'd prefer, or I'd endure,
rather than marry where love's not secure.

23

It's quite incomprehensible, I'm sure,
to man, that woman ever should refuse
offers of marriage. He feels so secure
of her, that he believes she cannot choose
but readily accept him when he woos.
Yet if to say 'Yes' she can hesitate,
it's better to decline the marriage state.

24

A sad propensity for being poor
afflicts the single woman, as a rule.
In matrimony's favour it's one more
strong argument—but only sways a fool.
I'd rather be a teacher at a school—
and I can really think of nothing worse—
than marry one to whom I felt averse.

25

Nothing, I feel, can ever be compared
to the dull misery of being bound
to one with whom the heart cannot be shared,
especially if love elsewhere is found.
Ah! then the torture will be most profound!
Woman's sole privilege is to love on,
longer than man, when every hope is gone.

26

Although there are such beings on the earth—
perhaps one in a thousand, scarcely more—
whose grace and spirit are combined with worth;
whose manners, heart, and mind we could adore
as all perfection; how can we be sure
a person of this sort will come our way?
Or, if he should do, be content to stay? . . .

27

And so I danced as I had done before
Tom went; and often had a pleasant night
when others fancied that the ball was poor,
or found no special reason for delight.
Enjoyment should make its own appetite.
I never found it worth my while to sit
and wait for *opportunity* for it.

 **IV**

Pleasures of dancing

One's consequence varies

An infusion of shrewishness

Man's heart unaffected by
costly clothes

———

28

What constitutes a good ball? you may ask.
—More dancers than the room can really hold!
To partner all the ladies is the task.
It's always melancholy to behold
a scarcity of men, both young and old,
with surplus women standing idly by,
and none to offer them civility.

29

Once there were twenty dances, and I danced
them all, and never felt the least bit tired.
Our ball was very thin that night. It chanced,
eleven ladies twenty men acquired.
'Twas everything the heart could have desired!
In winter, with few couples, I could well
dance for a week as for a half-hour spell.

30

Pray don't suppose that it was always thus.
At times I was but little in request.
One's consequence, you know, is various,
and for no reason swings from worst to best.
But I was just as happy as the rest,
and found enough amusement not to gape
till the last fifteen minutes—then escape.

31

One ball, of which I furnished an account,
my pen with shrewishness seemed to infuse.
No one was much admired save Mrs. Blount,
and her I found it easy to abuse:
the same broad face, pink husband, and white shoes!
Of Champneys' daughter I was critical—
I called her a queer white-necked animal.

32

The two Miss Coxes being there, I glanced
at both, and traced in one all that remained
of the broad-featured, vulgar girl who danced
eight years before at Enham; but I deigned
to praise the other. And I was constrained
to think a Mrs. Warren very fine—
regretfully—it was not by design!

33

To have new clothes for every gay event
my small resources sometimes overran.
One busy month my money was all spent
in buying white gloves and pink persian.
But not to look amiss was my chief plan.
Though dress distinction may be frivolous,
it occupies the thoughts of most of us.

34

Some ladies would be mortified to learn
of man's insensibility toward
the clothes they wear. Man only can discern
his brother man's inadequate regard
for costly, new attire. Alas, 'tis hard!
We think man's heart affected—though it's not—
by whether muslin's plain or bears a spot.

35

And though in mull or jackonet we shine,
man's unsusceptible upon this score.
For her own satisfaction woman's fine.
No man because of it admires her more;
no woman likes her better than before.
Neatness and fashion satisfy the male;
the shabby and bizarre with *her* prevail.

 V

Looking nice

Caps useful and caps for fun

Fruit, flowers and flat-heeled shoes

All colours and white

36

About fine clothes I never was a fool;
and yet that consciousness of looking nice,
which makes one look still better as a rule,
(such was the case, at least, with Fanny Price)
made me pay heed to fashion's least device—
as when I took Cassandra's bonnet's cawl
to dignify my own cap for a ball.

37

Although it must be many years ago,
that *nidgetty* black cap I still can see,
trimmed with a feather—was it coquelicot?
Mrs. Lefroy admired it much on me.
Caps were so useful, and I once made three,
just in the evenings when at home to wear:
they saved me worlds of torment with my hair.

38

But caps for going out were much more fun!
At Kempshott, Lady Dorchester's, that night,
Mary lent me her mameluke cap, the one
her friend Charles Fowle had sent her. It was quite
the latest vanity of fashion's height.
(Mameluke, you may recall, became the style
after the famous Battle of the Nile.)

39

A pretty cap that I liked very much
was one I bought in London from Miss Hare—
white lace and satin, with small feather such
as Harriot Byron was supposed to wear,
a white one perking out of the left ear.
Its narrow ribbon bows were full and large,
and One pound sixteen shillings was the charge.

40

Mrs. Lefroy and Martha wished to have
the pattern of the Austen caps one day.
This pleased me much. But when Cassandra gave
without the least demur the thing away,
I was not quite so pleased, I had to say.
A person's wish that is too soon content
may well give place to one less innocent.

41

I was at Bath in Seventeen-ninety-nine.
Both fruit and flowers were much worn that year.
Eliza's bunch of strawberries looked fine.
One could in grapes or apricots appear.
But at most shops the fruit was very dear:
three shillings for a greengage or a plum,
and five for grapes or cherries—what a sum!

42

As well as shopping for Cassandra's fruit,
and for friend Martha ordering flat-heeled shoes,
other commissions I'd to execute.
The little judgment that was mine to use
failed to enable me the best to choose,
except for Anna's stockings. Mary's veil,
imprudent purchase, made a sorry tale.

43

The veil was meant as a united gift
from both of us. I bought a muslin one
at half-a-guinea. This was wasted thrift—
thick, dirty, ragged, it would scarce have done
to show our brother's wife affection.
I changed it for another of black lace—
'twas sixteen shillings, but would not disgrace.

44

James Edward Austen-Leigh thought, far too young
my interest in fashion I'd outgrown.
He was mistaken. In my heart I clung
forever to the joy of a new gown,
as dear Lord Brabourne has so clearly shown.
From London, just three years before I died,
I wrote of my long-sleeved gauze gown with pride.

45

Lace, velvet, muslin, bombazine, or stuff—
I dressed in all, for I was tall and slim.
With my own needle I was skilled enough
to add a flounce, or change a ribbon trim,
or follow any other private whim.
Moreover, I sewed brother Edward's shirts
as neatly as I lengthened waists and skirts.

46

As well as sewing garments for the poor,
I sometimes worked a present for a friend.
The small chintz housewife that I made before
Mary left Deane, its contents all would lend
when she had caps and gowns to make and mend.
Hemming, or satin-stitch embroidery,
I often took up when my hands were free.

47

You'd like to know what colours I preferred?
I wore a lot of pink, and green, and blue,
and brown (dark brown), and yellow. In a word,
almost all colours of whatever hue.
But to give Edmund Bertram his just due,
and to prove sweet Miss Tilney in the right,
I think a woman looks her best in white.

 VI

Eating and drinking

Sponge cake and Stilton cheese

Mead and Madeira

Pride and Prejudice and pickled
cucumber

48

My obvious delight in things to wear
stands in my correspondence self-confessed.
With dear Cassandra I felt moved to share
my smallest plan of how I would be dressed.
But it was not my only interest.
I fear I wasted quite a lot of ink
on writing about things to eat and drink!

49

Dear Dr. Johnson says, Who does not mind
his belly, he will mind few other things.
The statement is a little unrefined,
and to its truth some party-spirit clings;
yet with sound commonsense the verdict rings.
For it was the good Lord's prerogative
to make us so that we must eat to live.

50

As readers of my letters long have known,
the purchase of a sponge cake was to me
just as exciting as the next new gown.
I was not subject to the tyranny
of every cherished family recipe
when keeping house, but would experiment
with all my appetite cared to invent.

51

We knew no lack of wholesome food at home,
such as keen, youthful hunger could appease;
and when we lived in lodgings, there would come
from many friends most welcome luxuries:
hampers of apples, half a Stilton cheese,
turkey, ham, hares, pheasants and venison—
pleasant reminders of dear Steventon!

52

I still recall devouring some cold souse,
one winter day when I was playing host
to Caroline and Anna at our house.
Which of the three of us enjoyed it most
is from my memory now, alas! quite lost.
But in my letter from the Rectory
I mentioned it to friends at Kintbury.

53

(Some friends of mine who went to Steventon
in Nineteen-sixty-seven could not find—
save for some broken rubble scattered on
the tangled grass—the least thing to remind
of all the happiness I'd left behind
when from my childhood home I'd had to part.
It ever held a warm place in my heart.)

54

Cassandra very often went to stay
with brother Edward at Godmersham. I
did the housekeeping while she was away.
I never found it hard to satisfy
my mother's standards, which were doubtless high.
My secret of success was to provide
the food which most appealed to *my* inside!

55

One day for dinner I had ragout veal;
haricot mutton on the morrow came.
An ox-cheek often proved a tasty meal,
with little dumplings in it—much the same
as the Godmersham people would acclaim.
Pease-soup, a sparerib, pudding, made no fuss
the day that Mr. Lyford dined with us.

56

My friends were ever most hospitable.
When on a visit once to Goodnestone,
my host's attention I remember well—
it was the sort of kindness always shown—
he made a point, on my account alone,
at suppertime of ordering toasted cheese,
because he knew how much the treat would please.

57

I often asked my friends to stay; and yet
sometimes the duties of hostess would pall.
Their going brought me comfort—and regret
I had not taken pains to please them all.
But constant care for meals could not enthral.
Rice puddings, apple dumplings, were to me
torments from which my soul longed to be free!

58

In our Southampton home one winter night,
sitting in a wide circle round the fire,
our shivers and our yawns turned to delight,
and our dull spirits rose a good deal higher,
when came the supper-tray, with much to admire:
the widgeon made a most delicious dish;
the candied ginger—all that one could wish!

59

I seldom knew my writing hand to shake
from port, liqueurs, Madeira, or French wine;
though I was not too scrupulous to take
a glass with friends or relatives of mine.
But home-made beverages were just as fine.
Currant and orange wine, mead, and spruce beer—
gallons of these we brewed ourselves each year.

60

At Chawton Cottage we grew strawberries.
Pleasure at finding them I still recall.
It was a joy to have our own green pease,
though our first gatherings were rather small—
not like the Lady of the Lake's at all!
But with two ducks from Wood Barn, I believe
they made a feast a king might well receive.

61

I cannot rival Arthur Parker's boast,
although I quite agree with what he said
about the vice and virtue of dry toast.
I am not one of those who are misled
to think it wholesome. Unless butter's spread
in reasonable quantities on it,
it irritates the stomach, I submit.

62

Unlike dear Emma's father, full rich fare
enchanted me; and I am sad to say—
though the occasion must have been quite rare—
a plate of mince pies I once sent away.
But I was rather headachy that day
at Mr. Pappillon's and I could eat—
except for jelly—nothing very sweet.

63

My brother Henry's housekeeper was French—
Madame Bigion. The dinners she prepared,
hunger the most omnivorous would quench.
And when those comfortable meals *I* shared,
no monarch at a banquet better fared.
One day in London she rejoiced my heart
with soup, fish, bouillée, partridge, apple tart!

64

At Edward's house, with my niece Fanny Knight,
I once remember dining upon goose.
I told Cassandra that I hoped it might
good sales for *Pride and Prejudice* produce—
edition number two. (It was my use,
often to utter nonsense such as that.
Please don't take literally my playful chat!)

65

At Chawton, eighteen months before I died,
I felt quite burdened with the household cares.
My relatives had troubles; love, or pride,
prevented me from adding mine to theirs.
My illness gained upon me unawares.
With joints and doses my poor head was full,
and composition seemed impossible.

66

Yet still I kept almost until the end
my interest in appetizing food.
Gifts came from many a relative and friend
who my few predilections understood.
James' pickled cucumbers—extremely good—
are still to me a memorable repast:
I'm thankful that I did not have to fast.

 VII

Allowed to read what books
I chose

The boundless pleasure of novels

Some favourite authors

Poetry and a torn petticoat

67

Though never one of Lady Russell's sort,
I could find endless pleasure in a book,
provided that the theme did not distort
those views of life that decent people took.
Such stories I confess I soon forsook!
But a good tale by fire or candlelight
was the chief joy of many a winter's night.

68

As Henry says, I was allowed to read,
from father's library, what books I chose.
His faith in me was too complete to need
the discipline a veto would impose.
Besides, who is the judge of worthwhile prose?
Parsons who read themselves *The Midnight Bell*
can scarcely claim such books lead straight to hell!

69

We were great novel-readers, all of us,
and not the least ashamed of being so.
Performances of wit, taste, genius,
the greatest powers of the mind they show,
and boundless pleasure on the world bestow.
Yet out of fashion, ignorance or pride,
no compositions are so much decried.

70

The masters of the novel-writer's art
I studied—Fielding, Richardson, and Sterne—
though Richardson came closest to my heart.
Often my thoughts to dear Sir Charles return,
and for that Cedar Parlour feel concern.
Its occupants were living friends to me
and lingered ever in my memory.

71

Most Gothic mysteries I found grotesque;
the tribute 'horrid' could not *me* beguile.
But Barret's *Heroine*, a gay burlesque
particularly on the Radcliffe style,
drew from me as I read it many a smile.
I was exceedingly amused by it,
and did not think that it fell off a bit.

72

The reader, who from my own work extracts
my favourite authors, places Johnson high
(though he dealt more in notions than in facts).
Some think my praise of Crabbe seems to imply
I'd have been Mrs. Crabbe without a sigh.
But Cowper, fond of tame hares and blank verse,
was for my love of countryside best nurse.

73

Shakespeare one gets acquainted with, without
exactly knowing how. He is a part
of every Englishman; so spread throughout
our life, that close to every mind and heart
are all the thoughts and beauties of his art.
It is our constitution's happy fate
to be with him by instinct intimate.

74

James read us *Marmion* by Walter Scott.
Ought I to have been highly pleased with it?
At first I told Cassandra I was not;
but later changed my mind, I must admit,
and made the poem a warm favourite
with Anne and Benwick, when the pair converse
on 'richness of the present age in verse'.

75

Scott did not put his name to *Waverley*;
yet when the book appeared I was aware
of its creator's real identity,
and told my niece, I thought it was not fair
that one who had already a large share,
from poetry, of profit and of fame,
riches from authorship should try to claim.

76

'Walter Scott has no business to write
novels, especially good ones,' I said,
'because from other people's mouths it might
take away every crumb of hard-earned bread.
He ought to keep to his own sphere instead.
Unless I cannot help it, I shall just
refuse to like his book—but fear I must!'

77

Poor Burns's known irregularity
hindered my full enjoyment of his lines.
I cannot separate the poetry
from a man's character. Though he enshrines
woman within his soul, my heart declines
to trust his feelings. Faith in them I've not:
he felt, and then he wrote—and then forgot.

78

I think that poetry can seldom be
safely admired by those who love it best.
They ought to taste it only sparingly,
who feel it fan the fire in their own breast.
Sometimes it filled me with a strange unrest . . .
I could not long o'er Byron's *Corsair* gloat,
but went and mended a torn petticoat.

79

By Sherlock's Sermons once I set great store;
to any others his I much preferred.
But evangelicals like Hannah More
somehow my inclinations rarely stirred.
Yet evangelicals—so I averred—
who are from reason and from feeling so,
may well be happier, safer, than we know.

80

When books of information came my way,
that could instruct as well as entertain—
like Captain Pasley's military essay,
or Carr's account of travelling in Spain—
a useful hint from them I'd sometimes gain.
Thanks to the latter, I could be precise
in a small matter touching William Price.

81

Miss Burney's *Evelina* long was first
among the novels that I most admired.
Within its leaves I often was immersed,
and of those 'wild-beast' Branghtons never tired.
That Holborn dinner-party was inspired!
Caroline heard me read it out one day—
she said she thought it sounded like a play.

82

It has, I hear, been stated that I took
the title of my *Pride and Prejudice*
from Fanny Burney's charming second book,
Cecilia. Where was the harm in this?
Writers exist by such small courtesies!
All who have read *Northanger Abbey* know
I paid my debt to Madame long ago.

83

Where 'Miss J. Austen' first appeared in print
was in 'Camilla's' grand subscription-list.
I saved the guinea for the book by dint
of self-denial. I could not resist
the third work of my favourite novelist.
Eleven hundred people felt the same:
among those great ones, mine was but a name.

VIII

Beginning to write

Sendups of silly novels and
scenes from plays

The fate of 'First Impressions'

'And so to Bath'

84

How young I was when I began to write,
or where, or why, I cannot now recall.
But I filled several copy-books with slight
and flimsy stories, which in general
were spirited, though quite nonsensical.
I exercised my youthful energies
on follies, whims and inconsistencies.

85

My most-praised early effort, as a rule,
is *Love and Freindship* (spelling is my own!).
It was my first attempt to ridicule
the sundry silly novels that are prone
exaggerated feelings to enthrone
without regard for truth. This must have been
before I reached the ripe age of sixteen.

86

Amongst the other fragments that I penned
about the same time were a scene or two
of plays I dedicated to a friend.
Theatricals to me were nothing new.
At Steventon each year we staged a few
out in the barn, and all the neighbourhood
thought our performances extremely good.

87

(In London once, when Miss O'Neil was cast
In *Isabella*, we were at the play.
I own—though not a real enthusiast—
my expectations she did not repay.
I kept my handkerchiefs both tucked away.
I fancy I want more than well can be . . .
But she hugged Mr. Young delightfully!)

88

A wish to be historian I nursed.
My sole accomplishment is still extant:
England from Henry Fourth to Charles the First
I sought to render more significant—
though 'partial, prejudiced and ignorant'!
But letters that I wrote for Cousin Jane
my self-expressiveness served best to train.

89

That brilliant books of letters might consist
I learned from Richardson. So I began
in the same form my work as novelist,
and thus wrote *Elinor and Marianne*.
A few years later I revised its plan.
Ere it was *Sense and Sensibility*,
the letter form had lost its charms for me.

90

When James's wife died, Anna came to stay
at Steventon. I helped amuse the child
with stories that went on from day to day,
for she was young, and easily beguiled.
Of 'First Impressions' I had then compiled
the first few chapters, which I read aloud.
Cassandra's pleased approval made me proud.

91

I finished this when I was twenty-one.
My father said the story read as well
as *Evelina*, for comparison,
and thought the manuscript would surely sell.
He offered to submit it to Cadell.
Merely to look at it the man declined.
I've since been glad that he was so unkind.

92

I soon began another book, my third.
The plot was partly set in Bath, the town
to which our home was soon to be transferred.
(The move was something of a wrench, I own.)
But to us all the place had long been known.
We had an aunt and uncle living there,
and often stayed with them for change of air.

93

The worst of Bath, some say, is that one meets
so very many ugly women there.
All the plain faces passing in the streets
seem out of all proportion to its share
of pretty women, and provoke despair.
For when *one* handsome face has come and gone,
thirty-five frights are sure to follow on.

IX

Lyme and the Cobb

Lord Tennyson and Louisa Musgrove

Lord Byron and the sea

Alas! Mrs. Lefroy . . .

94

From Bath we went exploring once to Lyme.
How wild we were with joy as we drove down
the long hill and still steeper street that climb
into the grandly-situated town!
We thought it justified its high renown.
A most strange stranger he, whose eye could trace
such charms, nor wish to know more of the place.

95

The walk that skirts the pleasant little bay
right to the Cobb; the Cobb itself; the line
of very lovely cliffs that stretch away
towards the east—these splendours all combine
to make a scene exceptionally fine.
We lingered long, and gazed, and scarcely bore
to tear ourselves away from the sea-shore.

96

(You may remember how Lord Tennyson
once paid a visit to the town of Lyme.
They thought he'd want to see the spot whereon
the Duke of Monmouth landed—so sublime
a souvenir from that historic time.
The poet cried, 'On *Monmouth* do not dwell;
but show me where Louisa Musgrove fell!')

97

All who deserve to look on it at all
feel glad, when to the sea they first return.
Lord Byron's 'dark blue seas' their hearts enthral.
They gaze and linger, as if to discern
remembered beauties, or some new one learn.
To watch a fresh breeze bringing in the tide
is a delight that cannot be denied!

98

No person can be permanently well,
though in good health he may appear to be,
unless once every year he goes to dwell
for six weeks at the least beside the sea.
The air and bathing act infallibly.
One or the other of them is a match
for all disorders that our bodies hatch.

99

The sea-air and sea-bath together bring
correctives for the stomach, lungs, and blood.
They're antiseptic, anti-everything!
They brace, or they relax, just as they should.
Strength, spirits, appetite, are always good.
Bathing's designed to cure, without the breeze;
the breeze alone, where bathing disagrees.

100

I felt my fortune had at last been made
when for ten pounds my tale of Bath was bought.
But in some dusty cupboard it was laid;
the publisher gave it no second thought.
(Though time his retribution duly brought!)
Some six years afterwards I tried again
to get my 'Susan' published—still in vain.

101

In Bath, life was not all of joy composed.
A sad blow fell upon our family:
dear father's virtuous, happy life was closed.
His death from suffering was almost as free
as we, his children, wished that it would be.
But loss of such a Parent must depress.
Who could do justice to his tenderness?

102

And so in Bath I could not really find
the heart to go on writing, or the will.
My first completed book had been declined;
my second paid for, but neglected still;
father was dead; my mother often ill;
while Mrs. Lefroy, best-belovèd friend,
in falling from a horse had met her end. . . .

 **X**

The loss of brother Edward's wife

What use are children?

The charms of Chawton Cottage

A warning door

———

103

A few years later, brother Edward's wife,
the lovely mistress of Godmersham, Kent,
bore an eleventh child, but lost her life.
Edward, who could no longer be content
to stay in that great, lonely mansion, went
to Chawton House, and was so generous
as to provide a cottage near for us.

104

(Too many wives are hurried to their tombs
by bearing an abundant family.
The simple regimen of separate rooms
is the best means to limit progeny.
Why don't more women try this recipe?
Poor animals! how else can they evade
a fate which makes them all too quickly fade?)

105

I do not say that children are no use.
Often when paying visits formally,
to easier conversation they conduce,
and yield, in cases of extremity,
a fruitful subject for the company.
But, on the whole, their charm is one that cloys:
prattle, and wilfulness, and tricks and noise.

106

My brothers' wives were blest with large increase.
Thirty or more times I was made an aunt.
I cherished every nephew, every niece,
with a warm love that nothing could supplant.
I let them know that I was vigilant
in keeping up an aunt's pre-eminence—
she was a person of some consequence!

107

Our Chawton Cottage opened on the street,
beside the village pond, quite close to where
the Winchester and Gosport highways meet.
We feared it would be rather public there,
because the passers-by could come and stare
in our front room; but this was much improved
when Edward had the parlour window moved.

108

Instead of looking out upon the road,
it opened now upon the garden side,
which made a more agreeable abode.
For though we had no mysteries to hide,
that we liked snugness cannot be denied.
The living-room still overlooked the street,
and often had to serve as my retreat.

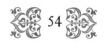

109

The garden was a joy to write about
in spring, when pinks, sweet williams, columbine,
and the syringas, too, were coming out.
(I loved these for the sake of Cowper's line.)
Our new-blown peony looked very fine.
The row of beech, the quickset hedge, did well.
The orchard walk had charms that none could tell.

110

(That my old Chawton home is now a place
of pilgrimage, which all the world can view,
to T. E. Carpenter, and to His Grace
the present Duke of Wellington, is due;
the Darnell sisters; and the steadfast few
who spent themselves so long and lovingly
in founding the J. A. Society.)

111

I'd had a dressing-room at Steventon
where I could write in solitary state;
but Chawton's room was used by everyone.
I could not always be so fortunate
as to be left secluded to create
the stories that were shaping in my brain;
and yet I felt that I could not refrain.

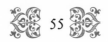

112

So at my writing-desk I often sat
and wrote, surrounded by the family;
though if a visitor called in to chat,
I'd slip all traces of my industry
beneath the blotting-paper instantly.
When anyone was coming, I was sure
of warning, by the creaking of the door.

 XI

Revising my old novels

'S. and S.' enriches me by £140

'P. and P.' sent down from London

Brother Henry praises 'M.P.'

113

In my old novels I was soon immersed,
and busily revised them for the press.
My *Sense and Sensibility* came first.
I gave the story a more modern dress,
and offered it with no small hopefulness
to Thomas Egerton, the publisher.
It sold quite well, but did not make a stir.

114

I stayed with brother Henry and his wife
in London, when the proofs were coming out,
and led a very gay, amusing life.
We entertained in Sloane Street; went about
to teas, and plays; Cassandra felt a doubt
if I was not forgetting 'S. and S.'—
a mother of her sucking child thought less!

115

The book was 'by a Lady', for I feared
myself as authoress then to proclaim.
But with it in the autumn list appeared
Maria Edgeworth's, Sarah Burney's name—
an augury, perhaps, of coming fame.
To fret at its reception I'd no grounds:
it made me richer by One-forty pounds.

116

This was, indeed, prodigious recompense
for that which had not cost me anything.
By it I was encouraged to commence
a new revision that more wealth could bring.
I worked at *Pride and Prejudice* next spring
(this was called 'First Impressions' earlier),
and sold it to my former publisher.

117

One January day I was quite wild
with joy, to have a set of 'P. and P.'
sent down from London—my own darling child!
I'd lop't and crop't it so successfully
that I at last imagined it must be
shorter than 'S. and S.'; though I admit
I still was vain and pleased enough with it.

118

The work was probably too light and bright;
rather too sparkling, also, I'm afraid.
The thing it needed most to put it right,
to stretch it here and there, and give it shade,
was a long chapter that good sense displayed—
or solemn nonsense—serving all the while
to form a contrast to the general style.

119

My mother read the novel to Miss Benn,
a neighbour who had dined with us that day.
She never dreamed the book came from *my* pen.
So great a secret we dare not betray.
She really seemed amused, I'm glad to say.
Unhappily my mother liked to read
with what I felt was rather too much speed.

120

Elizabeth she thoroughly admired.
With that delightful girl, how could she err?
When I created her, I felt inspired.
I must admit that I consider her
as nice as any printed character.
I do not know how I shall tolerate
those whom at least *she* fails to captivate.

121

And now another novel I began—
this was a new one, not an old revised.
It went according to my usual plan:
three or four country families comprised,
with village setting—though quite civilized.
Working on people placed in such a spot
always produces a delightful plot.

122

I asked my brother Frank to give me leave
the names of some of his old ships to use.
Something of fact with fancy thus to weave
was my ambition. He did not refuse.
(No woman could more generous brothers choose.
When Charles got his first prize, he spent his gains
buying us topaze crosses and gold chains.)

123

One day when I and brother Henry went
to London, driving thither by post-chaise,
the journey was most profitably spent
in reading *Mansfield Park* to him. His praise
removed all doubts that diffidence could raise.
He thought it not at all inferior
to the two novels that had gone before.

124

This book, again brought out by Egerton,
sold slower than I thought it ought to do.
Though I liked praise as well as anyone,
I liked what Edward christened 'pewter', too,
and wanted to increase my revenue.
By 'S. and S.' and 'P. and P.', my store
was now Two-fifty pounds—I longed for more!

 **XII**

My *Emma* published

The Prince Regent's librarian at
Carlton House

Emma dedicated to H.R.H.

Divers opinions of *Emma*

———————

125

I was at work upon another book
through most of Eighteen-fourteen and fifteen.
Not without some anxiety I took
a different sort of girl for heroine.
My Emma, I suspected, would not mean
as much to others as she did to me,
who always cared for her exceedingly.

126

To those who favoured *Pride and Prejudice*,
this book would seem inferior in wit.
Those for whom *Mansfield Park* might well suffice
would probably find less good sense in it.
Yet still I hoped the story would be fit
with my preceding works to take its place,
and what was good in them would not disgrace.

127

Though Egerton had been the publisher
of my three novels, no one thought it strange
when this time I decided to transfer
my work to Mr. Murray for a change.
So I went up to London to arrange
to meet the man who'd won himself a name
by propagating Byron's early fame.

128

Henry, unhappily, was sick in bed
when my new book was passing through the press.
He had a fever, needed to be bled,
suffered from chest pains and from biliousness.
A sudden crisis caused us much distress.
For several days he lay there gravely ill;
at last responded to the surgeon's skill.

129

This surgeon knew the Reverend J. S. Clarke,
custodian of the Prince's library
at Carlton House, beside St. James's Park,
the London residence of royalty;
and hither Mr. Clarke invited me.
The Regent, having heard I was in town,
kindly proposed this honour should be shown.

130

His Royal Highness had been pleased to state,
my novels he decidedly admired.
That to him therefor I should dedicate
Emma, seemed very much to be desired.
I would not, else, so highly have aspired!
But, sanctioned properly, I need not fear
presumptuous or ungrateful to appear.

131

The presentation copy for the Prince
found favour in a manner that perplexed;
for evidently he did not evince
as much consideration for the text
as for the binding. I was rather vexed
at being for a 'handsome' copy thanked:
the author much below the printer ranked!

132

Of *Emma* I was happy to receive
as many different views as I could get.
By them I was encouraged to believe
I had not overwritten myself yet.
The likelihood of doing so is met
by almost every author, soon or late,
who must depend on fancy to create.

133

Frank, for its air of nature, liked it more
than *Mansfield Park*, or even 'P. and P.',
although the latter had a greater store
of wit, the former of morality.
Likewise to Charles, the Woodhouse family
proved a delight, though *Pride and Prejudice*
had been his favourite novel before this.

134

'Better than "P. and P.", but not so well
as "M.P."', was Cassandra's estimate.
Mother still bowed to Mr. Collins' spell.
Fanny declared she could not tolerate
Emma; but Mrs. Cage was pleased to state,
she felt herself at Highbury all day.
I'm glad that everyone liked Mr. K.!

135

Miss Isabella Herries was quite sure
I'd meant the Bates for certain friends of hers—
people of whom I'd never heard before!
I wish to state that every reader errs
who finds live models for my characters.
Social proprieties thus to invade,
to me seemed no part of a writer's trade.

XIII

Invited to take a clergyman as theme

Confess myself unequal to the task

Likewise to that of furnishing
a historical romance

———————

136

Meanwhile the Reverend Mr. Clarke proposed
that I should take a clergyman as theme,
and write a book that his whole life disclosed—
all that he might be thought to do or dream.
I was not greatly flattered by the scheme.
I knew my limitations but too well,
and never sought outside them to excel.

137

What is the lot of those who choose the Church?
How is a clergyman to win success?
It is no use for him to go in search
of such distinctions as most men impress—
like heading mobs, or setting *ton* in dress.
In state or fashion he cannot be high;
yet his importance no one can deny.

138

And yet the charge he bears may be defined
as one of great responsibility:
all that's of first importance to mankind,
considered singly or collectively,
both temporally and eternally.
Our morals and religion he defends,
and on *their* influence our course depends.

139

Fine preachers may be followed and admired;
but in the parish, to be popular,
good principles and conduct are required.
The lack of these all usefulness would mar.
It will be found that as the clergy are
or are not what men think they ought to be,
so is the rest of the community.

140

Because he knows that human nature needs
more lessons than a weekly sermon gives,
the parish clergyman, who best succeeds,
among his own flock gladly works and lives.
He holds it chief of his prerogatives,
to their just wants and wishes to attend,
and prove himself their well-wisher and friend.

141

Some say that indolence and love of ease,
a want of every creditable aim,
taste for good company, of wish to please,
incline the clergyman to choose that game.
He's slovenly and selfish, so they claim.
His curate deals with all the work. In fine,
the business of his own life is to dine.

142

To do full justice to this theme would ask
much more ability than I possessed.
I felt myself unequal to the task,
and candidly my want of skill confessed.
Wide knowledge such a novel must attest,
of science, literature, philosophy.
I had no gift for much save comedy.

143

By the same gentleman I next was told
to furnish an historical romance
upon the subject of Prince Leopold
and Coburg, his august inheritance.
This would be timely, by the circumstance
of his approaching marriage to our own
young Princess Charlotte, heir to England's throne.

144

I could not seriously sit down and write
a serious romance, I said, unless
it was to save my life. If it were quite
essential, all amusement to repress,
before I'd finished Chapter One, or less,
I should be hung! I must go my own way:
in any other style, failure would lay.

XIV

Persuasion finished, *Northanger Abbey* regained, *Sanditon* laid aside

I leave home for ever

The final parting of the ways

———

145

In Eighteen-sixteen, sometime in July,
I brought my book *Persuasion* to an end.
One of the chapters did not satisfy,
and so two others in its place I penned.
I wrote to Fanny Knight, my niece and friend,
that she, *perhaps*, might like the heroine,
as Anne, for me, almost too good had been.

146

I thought this novel might perhaps appear
in the booksellers' list a twelvemonth hence.
Meanwhile my brother, later in the year,
bought back that tale of my Bath residence,
the fate of which had kept me in suspense
for thirteen years. He paid ten pounds, the same
as they had given—then revealed my name!

147

I was not really feeling like myself,
the first few months of Eighteen-seventeen.
In March I put *Northanger* on the shelf.
I could not say if my Miss Catherine
would ever by the reading world be seen.
I also laid aside my *Sanditon*,
though it was scarcely more than just begun.

148

In early spring of Eighteen-seventeen
the symptoms of my failing health increased.
I think my people could not have foreseen
how soon from life I was to be released.
My own firm hope of healing never ceased.
Yet when I went to Winchester in May,
I left my home 'forever and a day'.

149

But had I lived to be extremely old,
I'd not have known a better time to die.
My family's love and care cannot be told—
how their affectionate, warm hearts would try
each pain to soothe, each want to satisfy.
I would not very gladly have survived,
to be of so much tenderness deprived.

150

If ever you are ill, may you be nursed
as tenderly as I was. May the stress
by some alleviation be dispersed,
as mine, by kindly friends. May you possess—
as I daresay you will—the consciousness
of being not unworthy of their love:
so blest a feeling *my* heart could not move.

151

My dearest sister, tender, watchful, still
most indefatigable nurse of all,
was by her great exertions not made ill,
though hour by hour she answered to my call.
The debt I owed my loved ones—great or small,
I only could cry over it, and pray
that God would bless them more and more each day.

152

Cassandra's letters to dear Fanny Knight
have told the story of my last few days.
It is perhaps too painful to recite.
Yet all must reach this parting of the ways,
since life on earth is but a passing phase.
The 'treasured friend', the 'sister unsurpassed',
the 'other self'—all come to this at last.

153

Beneath a slab of marble, cold and black,
In Winchester Cathedral I was laid.
The mourners all went sorrowfully back
to their own homes. Religion lent its aid
to soothe deep grief that with the years would fade.
The bitter loss was borne with fortitude,
for Christian hope and faith each heart imbued.

 **XV**

Some compliments and criticisms

D. H. Lawrence and
a seven-letter word

My cheerful world is here for
all to share

———

154

Not many decades after I was dead,
to see my grave a friend once came from far.
'Pray can you tell me, sir,' the verger said,
'if there is anything particular
about that lady? She seems popular.
Dozens of folk who come to Winchester
ask me to point out where they buried her.'

155

Dear verger! happy with the well-filled pew,
whether the sitters stay awake or nod,
why should Jane Austen's name mean aught to you?
Her grave's but one of many you have trod
daily within this noble House of God.
I do not wonder that you should not know
why men before *her* stone pass to and fro. . . .

156

I hope you will not think me vain to quote
some of the charming compliments I've had.
For instance, there was Mr. Squire, who wrote:
'No one can be quite stupid or quite bad
who likes Jane Austen.' I need hardly add
that such a wise and tolerant decree
pleases me more than fulsome eulogy.

157

Sir Walter Scott, the least of flatterers,
admired the truth with which I could endow
all the involvements, feelings, characters
of ordinary life. *He* well knew how
to do what he once called 'the big bow-wow';
but lacked the finer touch which could invest
everything commonplace with interest.

158

Lord Morpeth, too, a handsome tribute paid;
(I quote *The Keepsake* with some diffidence!)
entitled me 'all perfect Austen'; said
that 'the dear Style flows on without pretence,
with unstained purity and unmatched sense';
declared the pleasure from my books derived
would last as long as memory survived.

159

The proudest author would not be disgraced
by Andrew Lang's kind estimate of me.
He said I counted everyone of taste
as my admirer. I alone was free
from women writers' lettered vanity.
In its reserve my art was delicate;
I did not force, insist, exaggerate.

160

Miss Brontë, though, despised my gentle style.
She thought me as a woman incomplete.
I did not ruffle nor disturb her; while
I dealt with human eyes, mouth, hands and feet,
not with the heart, of Life the unseen seat.
She said the Passions were unknown to me;
and could not help it, were this heresy.

161

That D. H. Lawrence loathed me, makes me glad:
'A most unpleasant person', he averred—
'English, I know, but only in the bad,
mean, snobbish sense of that seven-letter word.'
(Old maids were hardly things that *he* preferred!)
I welcome his remarks, however grim;
I should so hate to be admired by *him.*

162

Dear Dr. Chapman did not find me dull!
To track my thoughts, he travelled far afield,
with energy and zest incredible.
He made each page its inner secrets yield,
and did not rest till all had been revealed.
No writer had a more devoted friend:
I do believe he loved me to the end.

163

As for my present readers, most agree
that in my pages they forget all care,
sorrow, injustice, fear, perplexity,
and even war's gargantuan despair.
With those who need me most, I'll always share
my cheerful world. They shall not come in vain.
I'll take them to my heart, and ease their pain.

A Note on Rime Royal

Chaucer is credited with introducing this seven-lined stanza of iambic pentameter into our poetry; it was also used by Hoccleve, Lydgate, Henryson, Dunbar and Sackville. Shakespeare chose rime royal for *The Rape of Lucrece*.

Some authorities say it derives its name from the French *chant royal*; others, that it is due to James I of Scotland having chosen this form for *The Kingis Quair*, written in 1423 and 1424 when he was a prisoner in England.

The article, 'Verse', in the *Encyclopaedia Britannica* (1944 edition) describes rime royal as 'peculiarly English in character'.

Background

The Letters

Letters of Jane Austen, edited, with an introduction and critical remarks, by Edward, Lord Brabourne (Richard Bentley, London, 1884). The same in the 'Winchester' edition (John Grant, Edinburgh, 1912).

Jane Austen's Letters to her Sister Cassandra and others, collected and edited by R. W. Chapman (2 vols., Clarendon Press, Oxford, 1932).

The Novels

Sense and Sensibility, Pride and Prejudice, Mansfield Park, Emma, Northanger Abbey, Persuasion (all in Macmillan's Illustrated Pocket Classics series, reprinted from 1932 onwards).

Lady Susan ('Winchester' edition, John Grant, Edinburgh, 1912).

The Watsons (Clarendon Press, Oxford, 1927).

Sanditon (Clarendon Press, Oxford, 1925).

Other Sources

Biographical notice by Henry Austen prefixed to the first edition of *Northanger Abbey* and *Persuasion* (Richard Bentley, London, 1818).

A Memoir of Jane Austen, by J. E. Austen-Leigh, Vicar of Bray, Berks. (Richard Bentley, London, 1870).

Jane Austen, Her Life and Letters, by W. A. Austen-Leigh and R. A. Austen-Leigh (Smith, Elder, London, 1913).

Jane Austen, Her Homes and Her Friends, by Constance Hill (John Lane, London and New York, 1902).

Jane Austen: A Biography, by Elizabeth Jenkins (Gollancz, London, 1948 reprint).

Poets and Story-Tellers, by Lord David Cecil (Constable, London, 1949), especially pp. 97–122: 'Jane Austen' (the Leslie Stephen Lecture delivered in the University of Cambridge, 1935).

Abinger Harvest, by E. M. Forster (Edward Arnold, London, 1946 reprint).

A Miscellany, by A. C. Bradley, formerly Professor of Poetry in the University of Oxford (Macmillan, London, 1931 reprint).

Letters to Dead Authors, by Andrew Lang (Longmans Green, London, 1886), especially 'To Jane Austen'.

Talking of Jane Austen, by Sheila Kaye-Smith and G. B. Stern (Cassell, London, 3rd ed., 1947).

The Complete Novels of Jane Austen, with an introduction by J. C. Squire (W. Heinemann, London, 1928).

Evelina, by Fanny Burney, with introduction and notes by Annie Raine Ellis, editor of the early diary of Fanny Burney (Bohn's Library, London, 1881).

Memoirs of Dr. Burney, by Mme D'Arblay (Edward Moxon, London, 1832).

Jane Austen: The Critical Heritage, edited by B. C. Southam (Routledge & Kegan Paul, London, 1968).

Literature and Censorship, edited by H. T. Moore (Heinemann, London, 1955).

Phoenix II, by D. H. Lawrence (Heinemann, London, 1968).